Related to Loon

a first year teacher in Tuluksak

poems by

Jackie McManus

Finishing Line Press
Georgetown, Kentucky

Related to Loon

a first year teacher in Tuluksak

Copyright © 2021 by Jackie McMannus
ISBN 978-1-64662-530-7 First Edition
All rights reserved under International and Pan-American Copyright Conventions. No part of this book may be reproduced in any manner whatsoever without written permission from the publisher, except in the case of brief quotations embodied in critical articles and reviews.

Publisher: Leah Huete de Maines

Editor: Christen Kincaid

Cover Art: *Dipping and Diving.* Lisa Houck

Author Photo: Yvonne Pepin-Wakefield, Ph.D.

Cover Design: Elizabeth Maines McCleavy

Order online: www.finishinglinepress.com
also available on amazon.com

Author inquiries and mail orders:
Finishing Line Press
PO Box 1626
Georgetown, Kentucky 40324
USA

Table of Contents

Haiku 1

Letter to Peter and Matthew from Tuluksak 2

Flunking Nurauq 4

Not It 6

Haiku 7

Shibboleth 8

Cultural Mosaic 9

Honey Bucket Lambie Stories 10

Haiku 12

Church on the Kuskokwim 13

The Bell Ringer 15

Nome 16

Haiku 18

Electric Iqmik 19

Akutaq or A Poet's Obligation 20

Haiku 21

Related to Loon 22

Ptarmigan Hunting 24

Last Hunt 26

Haiku 27

Eskimoized Christianity 28

Climate Change 30

Note from Tuluksak 31

Haiku 32

For
Peter, Matthew, Bailey & Tucker

He swim me across
In a deep spot by the boat
We can't touch the sun.

Aima

Letter to Peter and Matthew from Tuluksak

Some part of me is frozen at the window. There's a green truck parked on our lawn at the end of the drive and you boys are throwing duffle bags and boxes in its open bed. What part of me had to act like it was just another morning? How I missed you already and you had not even left. I want to get this right, and never have. Now the guttural sound of the truck pulling away shakes the glass like a sheet of water. I open the back door, smoke a cigarette, two, look out to the woods. No wind. The smoke lingers and leaves me alone with an ache that was just too damn late. I wanted a name for what I felt but didn't deserve so I let that hang in the air, too. You were gone so I took it as a sign and moved to bush Alaska.

Today my first-grade class read around the room with pointers: one has a red apple on the end, another a pink heart, a green frog and still another, a gray elephant. Imagine that, an elephant in an Eskimo village. They had not even ever seen a cow until the year someone flew one in. But these are the things that stirred me: pointers and pens and scissors, paper clips, staplers, all the paraphernalia that must have made you ask *What the hell* when you opened the box I sent. Sorry. You were in college so I thought, but no, I did not think. It was my way to give pieces of me you had no use for.

For my first-grade students, I wrote sight words on pink tentacles of octopuses dangling from the ceiling and taped their names like clouds on the window, wall, or door. My second graders were coloring continents when the third-grade teacher stopped by. His eyes grew wide and his mouth opened because their maps are beautiful. I felt so proud of them. I'm proud of you, too, what it took to make a way, not a perfect one, but a way that would work.

I hope you are settling in, exploring Pullman. Your Uncle Jimmy's best friend, Jeff, showed me a forest trail, Kamiak Butte, where we stopped along the trail by an old log and took photos. The narrow dirt trail and wall of trees looked on farmland from the highest point around. You'll make it to Palouse Falls so loud with kolks and light. It almost drowns out that it's a destination for careless college harm. Your grandpa used to say *I think that's a bad policy.* Think about that. We're French Canadian and some say they named the Falls, Palouse: land of short and thick grass. In other words, lawn. My heart is broken for how I miss you and here I am in this small village with my small faith. Somehow, I just got used to losing.

Last Friday, someone broke into my house. I lock the door but that doesn't deter. Saturday some students arrived and I almost asked who stole the Little Debbie zebra cakes from my freezer. But the girls played in the bath-tub and later, the boys played dress-up with gowns and heels. Then there came a knock on my door. I heard them go silent, saw their dark eyes go wide and watched them scatter, a clumsy clicking of heels across the floor.

Sometimes when I wonder what I have done that is not a lie, this is what I remember: little Eskimo kids curled up with stories in the safe deep book-shelf of my living room, which was just big enough for three kindergarteners and cake. When it was time for them to go home, I told them I can't wait to see you at school in the morning. And it was true. And then I am watching the green truck disappear down the road, taking every true thing with it. It was as if I was fighting to get to you, past me, and all the dysfunction in my head.

I can't wait to see you, my boys. Enjoy your years at college. I remember my own college years, studying half the night the works of Campbell, Derrida, Milton, Hurston, the intellectual excitement of negative capability while you both slept, played, grew up. I loved everything about those years except how they kept me from you, all of me frozen at the window where you are not yet gone.

Flunking Nurauq

Perhaps the big mistake was flunking Nurauq.
After graduation, with one course on fetal alcohol
syndrome, I took a job on the tundra and became
an expert for a village two centuries old.

My PowerPoint slides for teachers and parents show
the smaller than normal brain of a six-year-old boy,
a tumbleweed of neural cells prematurely dead or slowed
in their migration through his developing brain, those

wide-set eyes, that thin lip. I watch their faces. They look
relieved by what they can do, terrified by what they can't.
There is a lull and as I wait someone slips me a piece
of torn paper: Nurauq, it says.

It is the beginning of the year. Of eight second graders,
two seem like seven-year-old alcoholics trying to stay sober.
Sometimes, the girl curls up in a corner against the cabinet
where I store paint sets and glue, her wide eyes scan

the room from the floor. Once, the principal's wife
had a native aide remove her. The grandmother paused her
Yup'ik lessons to witness the wild flailing, the incoherent
cry. Yet she becomes my best student. But a sweet river

in one boy's veins veered north through harsh land.
I imagined he felt like the longest river in the world. Before
school began, Nurauq was on his way home from fish camp
where he worked and played near the confluence of two rivers.

I can hear those rivers. I know the fish they hold, how
they feed a village. I see in his smiling eyes the emptiness
of a world that will always lift its glass. Cheers, his face says.
Perhaps the big mistake was flunking Nurauq,

because when the sun disappears for months and snow buries
the village and even when the sun appears and ice breaks up,
school lacks relevance led by *kass'aqs who do not speak
the language or live the same life, who vanish come summer.

Perhaps the big mistake came fifteen years earlier and thirty
miles away in an Eskimo trading center with a new cash
economy. Commercial fishing and bootleggers delivering
liquor by air with the now ready cash which brought violence,

which brought crime, which left kids somersaulting
through poisoned water. I return again and again to the child
behind the drink, to this talk given for the three district's
schools, twenty miles apart on the tundra. The rule

is to show and not tell so I've come with my slides and data.
Afterward the villagers show me fish heads buried outside
the door for the delicacy called stinkfish. They serve a lunch
of caribou and akutaq. The next day hungry kindergarteners

arrive at school high on iqmik for breakfast. They've walked
from two-bedroom homes shared by three handfuls of relatives
to learn, but mostly to eat. I stood before staff in an over-
equipped school that did not teach Eskimo history

or life studies for the Eskimo. I stood as a first-year teacher
having taken one multicultural class, representing
one model: the white world.
And the big mistake was flunking Nurauq.

---

*whites/non-Natives

Not It

Arrssuyaq gave me the first-grade assignment at the Anchorage job fair
but two months later I arrived in the village where the white principal
said first grade will be taught by my wife

so I became the reading teacher (without the reading teacher's salary)
which is why I was sitting in the third and fourth grade classroom
that first day of school.

Another first year teacher sat at his desk as if he did not see students
playing a game of tag they called Not It. Some darted from wall
to wall, some folded their bodies beneath wooden desks,

a handful at the window tried to climb out. Tomorrow a bookshelf
would block it, but today students stepped on chairs to reach the sill,
then ran to corners, bouncing off before

sprinting away. I laughed then because I didn't know what else
to do. Their teacher frowned a proselytizing frown. I took
my neatly typed lesson plans and walked toward the kindergarten

to see if I might teach, but tiny children flew out its two doors.
Some had collaborated to push a kidney-shaped table
near the window, and I knew then: this had been done before.

From wall to window, children ran. Three hid under their teacher's
desk while she chased others with two native aides. Soon, the principal
and secretary arrived to help. They were balls of ebullience

and I wanted to walk right out of that moment, except, I enjoyed it
too much. In the farthest village on the tundra, accessible by boat
or plane when accessible at all, enclosed by woods and river

and running children, I played this year's game of Not It. Later, I sat
with the teachers inside the school. We opened our mouths to speak,
and like hundreds of staff on the tundra before us, nothing came out.

*Camp on the mountain
Picking berries, black, blue, red,
Orange. Salmonberries.*

Callerkua

Shibboleth

The cab driver from the Anchorage airport glanced
in the rearview mirror several times before saying
We're being followed. How could we be followed?

Earlier, when the stewardess asked the name of the village
where I would teach, I went blank but offered,
It starts with a T. *You must mean Tuntutuliak*, she said

but who knew? It was after dinnertime and dark.
The cab driver took back roads for miles with sharp turns.
Somehow, we arrived.

The motel resembled our ride so I tipped a wooden chair
beneath the rickety doorknob, ran my daughter a bath,
wrote postcards home.

The next morning we boarded a Cessna bush plane
in winds that felt like thirty knots and gusts that shoved us
to one side, then another, like corners taken in a cab.

My daughter watched for moose on the tundra.
The high school English teacher waited near the sedge-
lined runway and if I had known anything at all about

love, I would have found that, sometimes, it isn't a
mistake. The school secretary gave us Yup'ik names.
My daughter with her blonde hair and blue eyes became

Atsacuaq, Little Berry, and we thought of cloudberries,
salmonberries, golden-berries, berries that reminded us
why, berries that said one can't live for nothing.

My Yup'ik name was Atsarpak
and I keep saying it wrong so it means Big Belly.

Cultural Mosaic

As the villagers talk, I listen for suffixes that bind to a root word,
                that forge meaning the length of a full sentence.
The first word I try is my name, and I say it incorrectly.
                This is how easy it is to lose a language.
They listen and smile. Close enough, they say.

Uyaquk, the shaman turned missionary, devised a script
                one hundred years before I arrived. I imagine
he saw village schoolchildren at the turn of the century,
                their mouths taped shut,

so he staked a claim on the Yup'ik language and wrote it down.

I hear the elders say These are not my words, not because
              they are not their words but because the words are old,
because the words are sacred, their words the words of ancestors.
              Elders names once bequeathed to the newly born

now bear Christian names like Mary, Joseph, Peter.

They graft a foreign language onto the syntax of their own,
              as they accommodate, assimilate, and adapt.
They eat traditional akutaq and stinkfish,
                  but with chips and pizza.

They dress like Americans.

Honey Bucket Lambie Stories

It is October when the pipes freeze.
Our home on Teacher Housing Road
built on wooden pilings low set
to the permafrost beneath it.

That winter a villager brought a white
five-gallon bucket he emptied daily
for months in the honey pit.

I can see my four-year-old daughter,
black sequined *qaspeq and conical hat,
sucker in her hand that grips
the plastic rim of the pail, glass beads

off her seal boots dangling against it, elbows
locked to her thin side. I sit criss-cross
applesauce on the tile floor beside her.

Once upon a time, I began,
(to distract her from the rim's rough edge)
there was a lambie.
(Oh Lamb of God please fix our pipes.)

And there was a wolf named Princess,
the heroine of a mountain, and an evil wolf
who does not have a name.

Lambie's mother cautions her,
Play close to home. Do not wander off.
Her best friend, Grace, would remind her,
too, but inevitably she would go,

sometimes with Grace, along the steep trail
seeking dinosaurs she thought she saw once
or heard of once, she can't remember.

---

*traditional hooded shirt

They were always Tyrannosaurus Rex
dinosaurs, and she would always see them
dancing in a meadow on some furtive spot,
their tiny arms full of a confetti

of light and leaves and mountain mist
that would lead her to blink her eyes,
to exclaim, they are real.

Each time before she could join them,
the bad wolf who does not have a name
would show up. He would be just off trail
waiting for opportunity

and she would be in sudden trouble:
What other kind is there?
In every story Princess materialized

to save her and to say for the ten
hundredth time, stay close to home.
Nine years later, she wandered off.
She hitchhiked to places where

there was an evil wolf with many names
but there was a princess, too,
and dress-up clothes

and a grace that held the shape
of someone bent like a monk,
the weight of story on his hands,
soiled with ice and piss.

*Two swings by the church.
I go home after school. I
swing by the white church.*

Nuqarr

Church on the Kuskokwim

A congregation of villagers,
                teachers, mothers, fathers,
and a trellis of kids
packed into an open skiff
to go to Kwethluk to sing.

At five o'clock,
                after two church services
and three meals,
we piled back in the boat
just in time

for thunder, rain, lightning.
                Showers
in slow waves across the delta.
We could see to the horizon
in all directions from Kwethluk.

Bottoms of clouds in the northwest,
                commandment black,
with their edge and top
the shade of pale stone.
The sun sank further until

the wind-whipped sky became
                an uncertain hue
like low bush cranberries
pulled by a lone cloud
opposite the sun, and resurrecting pink,

the color of broken river ice
                and trout.
A maelstrom of light
fell over the boat
from clouds ridiculously vivid,

and a preaching rainbow pillar
                              shot
straight into its black base.
The weight of the sky lifted
as the men navigated a high prayer

of waves and wind
                    at forty miles an hour,
the speed of holy,
pelted and drenched and home by ten thirty,
baptized to the bone.

The Bell Ringer

They asked him to church on Low Sunday to ring the bell
        at two o'clock. But at twelve-thirty the presbyter thought
maybe the bell ringer was still using old time; it might be two o'clock,
old time.

And today there is news. A father, a husband, found
        hanging among the slim trees on the edge of the village—

the same trees a pilot did not clear from the end of the dirt runway,
the same trees an overstory,
the same trees that will bear the weight of next Sunday's hymns—

those trees.

And maybe no one saw him lug the wet rope to the woods.
        Who is to say, by hand or by foot, when the clapper strikes
the leather pad on the bell,

what is the reason?

At seven o'clock the bell ringer was still on old time
and life tried to go on.

When the villagers heard the half-muffled Sunday knell
it was, they thought, ten o'clock, Quasimodo time,
but it was actually almost eleven.

The wrong time, the time it took, the timing.

The bell ringer can decide it is any time he wants it to be.
        What time is it now, surely he asked himself,
dragging the braided rope through the mud, throwing it over
        the branch of a tree, tugging it down

to catch the sally
 and tying a uni-knot, he left the field of time,
        swinging like a pendulum.

Nome

The high school English teacher and Tuluksak church
singing group, which doesn't have a name, rode in the back
of a villager's pickup down the wild long lonely Kuskokwim
through shell ice and blowing sand forty miles to the airport

where they chartered a nine-passenger plane for four thousand
dollars. It was a pretty flight, low clouds hiding the mouth
of the Yukon. In Nome there was someone to pick them up.
This surprised everyone. It was a good time

to be in Nome. Mushers finishing the Iditarod
while men on either dogsled or snowmachine hit orange
golf balls into coffee cans embedded in sea ice for a six-hole
tournament on a sunny, windless, minus ten-degree day.

When the siren sounds, they had ten minutes to get to Front
Street. When the siren went off, the high school English teacher
went to see the mushers coming in. It wasn't all that exciting,
he said, but it was something to do. The Tuluksak church

singing group knew mushers from the fast and icy
Kuskokwim 300 that stops in their village, and while they
talked and gathered autographs, the high school English teacher
had his head measured around the top, under the chin,

and from eyebrow to eyebrow, and from eyebrow over the top
to the hairline for a custom hat of spotted seal and sea otter.
The hat cost more than the trip but it was art and it is a good hat.
There was singing and witnessing in Nome. Church

was a fancy church, not the Moravian one falling off
its foundation on the swampy tundra. The high school
English teacher had never been to a "holy roller" service,
and definitely was not expecting Yup'ik holy rollers.

For years the Yup'ik church he knew, restrained,
the music a toned-down Southern Baptist hillbilly mix.
Now overwhelmed when people shouted, rolled on the floor
and spoke in tongues, it was about as unYup'ik as anything

he could have imagined. Fortunately, the service lasted only
seven hours. It would have gone longer but they were starting
to worry that food prepared for afterward would spoil.
Forty people came to eat. Sourdough pancakes, caribou, rabbit,

salmon soup, and muktuk. They ate so well they did not once
have to go to Burger King. The six-foot tall high school English
teacher, worn out from worship and offered the lumpy five-foot
long couch at four a.m., took a spot on the floor that was not taken.

He had to ride in the back of the pickup again.
The driver stopped in Kwethluk for a song service
at the Moravian church.
Everyone was falling asleep, yet the presbyter spoke...

*...The darkness of the world is filled with temptation
that puts a skin over our eyes. Open our eyes to the truth.
Let us not fall asleep as others do, but let us keep awake
and be sober...*

but they fell asleep anyway, so the driver drove eighty miles an hour
up the ice road of the Kuskokwim, plowed by a thirty-year-old plow
truck they named Tumlista, Yup'ik for 'the One who makes the Trail,"
bought off Craigslist from the Seattle-Tacoma airport.

And after tribes drilled thousands of holes in the living ice that is born,
matures as thick as five feet, and dies, maybe the road reaches the river's
mouth at the Bering Sea, and isn't it just like real America, they said,
smoother than your average freeway and quite comfortable.

Shooting moose in trees.
We bring the moose to our house
Pumping gas to cook.

Atuk

Electric Iqmik

Sometimes the men use a hammer
to knock the fungus free
from a decaying birch.

Sometimes they mix it by hand with tea.
Sometimes a blender grinds the punk to a finer ash
and the body absorbs it like a sponge.

They chew the powdery ash with tobacco leaves.
The youngest man sits down, dizzy, then throws up.
It is his first time.

Ten pounds for two hundred fifty dollars
of punk ash straight from Tuluksak.
Cut it, crush it, blend it, snort it,

smoke it, chew it, and with a little tobacco,
it lasts longer. They say it is supercharged
with taste like a smoldering campfire.

White teachers smell it and grieve
kindergarteners who are high while
native mothers lament their babies

cry if denied. In the village, small
slurping sounds as girls storyknife,
chewing tobacco fungus, its shape

the shape of ears. Black spit
hits the ground where teaching stories
inhabit the earth.

Akutaq Recipe or A Poet's Obligation

Use one cup bird fat,
or tunuq, that hard tallow from moose, reindeer or caribou
or one cup Crisco, and if it is the right season

if you live where it snows in June,
add two cups loose snow. Or add water.
Akutaq means mix together. Akutaq.

Use four cups, five cups, a gallon of berries!
It is a life decision, a family mark to use the same berries,
to keep your social standing

but those are the old ways
and when I make this ice cream, I have no old ways
or social standing. Putting blessings before hardship,

mix cloudberries, blueberries, raspberries, mossberries.
Optional: nuts and raisins.
Tradition says, add ground fish. Some say the taste

sans meat is too sweet like using canned fat instead
of fresh fat from the tundra. And even though the men say
sweet fish is foolish, stir in sugar until dissolved.

Beat. Use large circles until foamy and thick.

I watched an elder trace a cross on her akutaq.
She chose one berry with a pinch of blubber
from the fat of the tundra bird, turned

and tossed it in the campfire, then spoke out
my only obligation:
Tamarpeci nerculi. "All of you, eat."

Hunting white rabbits
It keep hopping by the lake.
We had a hard time.

Inaqa

Related to Loon

Once I bought a postcard of a lone road, its endless curve
of asphalt with the caption, "Bend in the road." Later I went
to an Eskimo village, its meandering rows of rough wood homes

along the gravel bar of a slow river, how it made a long arc
to meet the mighty Kuskokwim like traveling down that barren
postcard road and, all of a sudden, seeing a town.

Tul'yagmyut means related to loon, yet I saw no loons on
the tree-less plain of ponds and peat and tussock grass,
the alluvial land a hush. Once I thought I heard its shuddering wail

like some startled lost scream in the middle of a logjam. Imagine,
nothing for miles and then a nest of wood: school building, post office,
laundromat, church, as if stranded on too small a lake

like a loon trying to lift its solid bones from water but needing
the length of an airstrip to do it, and then, its early summer calls
across the tundra: hear me, find me, help. It was early summer, too,

when the kindergarten teacher stood at my door, weapon in her hand
at one a.m. Her large frame blocked the moon that glinted off
the metal rivets of a six-inch steak knife held in her fist.

She had left her Mormon roots in the lower forty-eight so we drank,
knowing it could get us kicked off this bend in the road.
We talked about yuraq, the dancing, drumming, singing, how

we asked what does it mean and felt the children's gaze
anchor to the only ground they knew while it eroded around them.
(It's possible we were naive kass'aqs.)

We wrestled *yuuyaraq with a naive blend of faith and doubt, and
because we didn't know what else to do, we held it snug beneath
its low-slung neck with lesson plans and the heart of a loon

trying to stay afloat long enough to matter. Loons will fight
for turf, yet where are the loons in Tul'yagmyut? Only broken
fathers, cowardly uncles, and a bend in the river

flowing proud in the blood of an indigenous people who believe
they are the river, except at my door, a territorial white teacher
from Utah is saying, let's go get them. We felt before we heard

short piercing tremolos across the delta, children, absorbing the
sound of the loon. You're going to need a sharper knife, I said,
to carve this loon, and everyone said you can't save a village,

which made us fierce until it made us tired. A school siren in
the morning became the wailing river, became the brooding tundra
sky, an extension of our dreaming as we felt the pulse

of permafrost beneath us. And we knew at any minute, how just
when you are about to fall asleep or when your hand is about to relax
and sheath the knife, there would come the rapid quack of the loon
                                to *snap* you awake.

---
*way of living

Ptarmigan Hunting

Last week the math teacher went ptarmigan hunting with Yaqulpak. They spent a lot of time on snowmachines looking for black bear, but the odds of finding a bear are slim, and the odds of finding ptarmigan

are high, so they were ptarmigan hunting. They were expecting to be out until ten but had to chase some caribou for a while. Yaqulpak did not want to shoot a caribou but they still had to chase them around

a little, and all of a sudden they were a lot closer to the mountains than they had meant to go. Snow had blown from the high plateau to the tundra floor that folded and slumped into a mosaic of streams

on the frozen plain. Yaqulpak decided they should cross those streams to get home. The whole trip when they went through water he would say Don't worry, these aren't real rivers; They aren't very

deep. This time he looked at the stream and said Even though they aren't real rivers, some of them are deep. Walking out on a beaver dam, he cut away upvigaq, the bog willow protruding too high, and

ptarmigan-pecked twigs pointing the wrong way, then mounted his machine. The first stream they crossed was shallow. The next one will be harder, but they don't know that yet. Troublesome looking

ice hugged the beaver pond side. Water flowed around the far end, deep enough, wide enough. The real problem was not all beavers, but this beaver, on this stream, this tundra. He was an ecosystem

engineer. He broadened the small stream, deepened it, had already helped thaw the permafrost. Skis above water, they spooled up that final fifteen feet. Yaqulpak got through and came back to make sure

the math teacher had made it. Yaqulpak never comes back to make sure you make it. On the last beaver dam, his skis did not clear water, sticking straight up, the front of the machine submerged. They heard

the sound of ptarmigan wings in flight, their reedy cluck echoing over the five-hundred-pound snowmachine, tangled in cayuggluk, a scramble of dwarf birch, and its cousin, meadowsweet and thick

arctic moss. They could not get in the hole to lift without sloshing
waist-deep in freshly thawed water. This was all new and exciting
to the math teacher. He had a good idea where they were. While

they roped the snowmachine to a tundra anchor, pointed its skis
sideways, rocked it loose from its entanglement, packed the snow
down, and pulled and lifted, the math teacher thought: all three

of the streams with beaver dams flowed slowly south. These
might form one larger stream. He knew they were between
the streams and the Tuluksak River. Those circuitous waters

must drain into the river between where they were and where
they could get off that floral-rich, water-saturated tundra, toward
home. He was curious how Yaqulpak was going to cross that large

stream when they came to it. Sometimes a person must decide:
Is it wiser to go ahead or go back? Steep banks on both sides
had twenty feet of snow that left thirty feet of flowing water

in the middle. Yaqulpak saw a spot where the bank on their side
was less steep. It looked like you could get up the other side.
He used the axe to check the depth of water and declared it not deep.

They hit the water as quick as they could go in that short a space.
The water was deep. They were going fast enough to skip across
when Yaqulpak got stuck roaring up the bank. Time passed viscous

and slow to untether machine from boggy tundra, then moved quick
with hope they were past all obstacles between them and home.
Ptarmigan wings marked the snow, their feathered snowshoe feet,

their long claws, scratches in the snow, then flight. Yaqulpak's wife
was worried but they were home by midnight, so they didn't know
why she would have been worried.

Last Hunt

The caribou are pouring in. It is like a dream
except they are eating all the lichen.
So I walked to the tundra with the high school
teachers to shoot a caribou.

I shouldered the .270 like a purse
and walked toward the Kilbuck Caribou
Herd. I meant to observe Yup'ik tradition,
giving my caribou meat to the village

in exchange for good karma, but the herd
scattered and they ran as fast as antelope.
I thought I had to shoot my gun
at least once.

The shop teacher was walking back from
where he downed a bull when I glimpsed
a set of antlers behind him. I pressed
the stock of the gun to my shoulder,

placed the crosshairs low, took a deep breath,
slipped off the safety, and squeezed.
The shop teacher lowered his head
but kept his eyes dead on me,

as if asking what he should not have to ask.
I stepped behind a bush to pee, slung
my rifle back like a shot of whiskey
and went home.

*I went for a walk
looking for brown birds to sling
here in Tuluksak.*

Alek'aq

Eskimoized Christianity

In the fall of 1794 eight Russian monks
felt charged by God to lift the natives of Alaska
out of barbarism into civilization which meant
cleanliness, industry, Christianity—not in that order.
Their timing was good. American whalers

took walrus and seal, porpoise and cod but left
disease when caribou herds were low, when fish
supplies were low. And the river communities
hungered.

Some missionaries were murdered by the Eskimos
they were trying to save, others became distracted
by teaching duties and reindeer management. Some
turned their Laodicean cant for God toward gold,
which made the church ask: Should we proceed

or retreat? Headed for Siberia a few years after,
a Swedish priest got lost, ending up in the village
of Unalakleet where he hid under the house
of Nashalook three months, and we don't know

if Nashalook knew he was there until with a stroke
of luck, the Swede saved the life of Uyaraq, called
Rock. Just a teenage boy, fatherless and foolish
but with a little English and a lot of prompts,
Rock became the Swedes interpreter,

and they prayed up and down the delta
in competition with the shamans for native souls.
When he came there were no Christians;
When he left there were no heathens.

By 1910 you could not find an Eskimo
who was not a Christian Eskimo. But the wall
between the physical and the spiritual is not
that thick. It is not even a wall. There was some
serious backsliding. The Eskimos tried not to drink

and tried not to dance and tried not to smoke,
but Thou shalt not smoke was not in the Bible
and Ecclesiastes said it is time to dance and be merry
supported by Apostle Paul, Drink no longer water

but use a little wine. And that was that. Missionaries
brought medicine but took away shamans, brought drink
but took away dance, brought language but took away
ceremonial names, brought tools and skills to bolster belief.
And yet. Bad hunting and death, sickness and conflict

counted on an old credence, a practice rooted in fear.
What they could hide from the priests, they could not hide
from the sorcerer. In this way, together, they combined
the new religion and the new way without rejecting the old.
And it spread like the flu.

Climate Change

Today a letter arrives. In it the music teacher says
he ripped his CDs onto his hard drive so songs
play at random. It might be Ray Charles or Dolly

Parton but this time, years later, it's Nanci Griffith's
"Don't Forget About Me." He says he visited Everin
Nick's family last week. Wipe your nose before

you come in, they told him. And I can see him smile
because Everin Nick is making fun. They had been
confined to the village on a late November day,

the river viscous, but still not cold enough to freeze
for travel. Look at the waters of the river, they said,
studded with pink salmon floating downstream

in too warm waters, their one eye resigned to see,
and it is enough to wish your nose run from bitter cold
and fierce tundra wind. *Ngev'uq, and they laughed

a patient almost conspiratorial laugh, then looked
out at the polygon shapes of permafrost, at the salmon
expiring in plain sight and the God-haunted ground

melting beneath the village until Everin Nick shook
his head, stared at his hands, at the cracked palms,
and turned his hands over and held them.

I always remember, he writes, our trip to the nearest
village thirty miles away, how that year the river froze
by Thanksgiving, and how that was the last time.

---
*he blows his nose

Note from Tuluksak

Thomas and two third grade Asulaq boys tried to burn down the school. We had just returned from an inservice to find flames and the principal's wife outside with her daughter and a friend, their faces black. The librarian tore through the school ripping fire extinguishers off walls. Last year it was Joe-Joe and another first grader. Every year: same fire, different grade level.

We start school Wednesday. The Yup'ik say bad weather hunts someone, so the biggest difference for the start of school is we have good weather. A little sunshine helps to get things started right. Everyone is here, setting up classrooms. The first-grade teacher's replacements' replacement arrived in Bethel. The principal went to pick her up but the suburban broke down, so that needs replacing, too. There are not a lot of changes, which is a surprising change.

School has hardly begun and next month the male students leave for a moose hunt. Hairyman, the Alaskan Yeti, was spotted near the Tuluksak River at the last hunt. They said it threw rocks at them and stole their axe from camp. Some said it must have been a moose but the students said moose have a neck that bends like a man and they don't throw rocks or steal your axe. This morning the new teacher stepped over a male student on her path to the printer, so he is worried he will have bad luck on the hunt.

In spring, the female students leave to hunt duck, geese, and ptarmigan eggs. There is flat land to the east. One family egg hunting at Kasigluk saw Hairyman walking toward them, his long arms pendulous until he saw them, stiffened, and turned away. They found fruit stacked in pyramids like a grocer and thought Hairyman stacked them but Hairyman usually just robs fish from village smokehouses. Elders say he comes down from the third peak of the Kilbuck Range and doesn't do anything really, just takes and eats, so we don't have anything to worry about.

Mountains in soft snow
Nicholai climbing and me
We hear quiet planes.

Tupilluk

Note to Reader

I taught school in the Eskimo village of Tuluksak, Alaska where I learned and used my first two Yugtun words: aqumi (sit down) and taikaa (come here). My gratitude goes to the first and second grade children I was lucky enough to teach, for their patience and humor and joy. They worked diligently through many lessons to create the haiku included here.

I am grateful to the village community that welcomed me, helped me, protected me, and to native and nonnative teachers alike whom I was privileged to work with. I carry your stories with me, have not forgotten any of it, and only regret leaving too soon. I did not realize how much it all meant until I was gone. Not all poems are entirely factual but they all have one foot in fact based on my experience. Names have been changed throughout the book for anonymity.

I am grateful to Kathleen Flenniken, BJ Hollers, Karla Huston, and Dale Brandenburger for their initial readings and kind support. Thank you to Bailey McManus and Bobby Casey for tweaking the storyknife image found after each poem. A heartfelt thank you also to my two critique groups. I could not have done it without you. My sincere appreciation to Sky Island Journal for publishing the poem "Church on the Kuskokwim."

Lastly, I am grateful to family who tolerated my absence, especially my two sons away at college during this time. Much gratitude to my daughter who took on the Alaskan adventure with me and to her father who missed her. To my family then, and to the people I met during this time in the village, *quyanaqpak.

---

*thank you very much

Jackie McManus published a book of poetry, *The Earthmover's Daughter*. She has been published in *Sky Island Journal, Thimble Literary Magazine, Cathexis Northwest, Front Porch Review, VoiceCatcher, Barstow & Grand, MAW, Gorge Literary Journal, Q/A-a poetry journal, Volume One, The Stanley Republican, The Green Light Literary Journal*, and received an honorable mention from The Oregon Poetry Association. You can also find her poetry on the Washington Poetic Route map, a digital endeavor of former poet laureate, Claudia Castro Luna. She is at work on a forthcoming poetry chapbook and a memoir co-written with her daughter, Bailey McManus.

Please consider leaving a review on finishinglinepress.com or amazon.com.

www.ingramcontent.com/pod-product-compliance
Lightning Source LLC
LaVergne TN
LVHW041557070426
835507LV00011B/1130